Every Kid's Guide to

Understanding
Human Rights

Written by

JOY BERRY

Waco, TX 76710

About the Author and Publisher

Joy Berry's mission in life is to help families cope with everyday problems and to help children become competent, responsible, happy individuals. To achieve her goal, she has written over two hundred self-help books for children from infancy through age twelve. Her work has revolutionized children's publishing by providing families with practical, how-to, living skills information that was previously unavailable in children's books.

Joy has gathered a dedicated team of experts, including psychologists, educators, child developmentalists, writers, editors, designers, and artists to form her publishing company and to help produce her work.

The company, Living Skills Press, produces thoroughly researched books and audiovisual materials that successfully combine humor and education to teach children subjects ranging from how to clean a bedroom to how to resolve problems and get along with other people.

Managing Editor: Ellen Klarberg
Copy Editor: Annette Gooch
Contributing Editors: Libby Byers, Nancy Cochran, Maureen Dryden,
Yona Flemming, Kathleen Mohr, Susan Motycka
Editorial Assistant: Lana Eberhard

Art Director: Jennifer Wiezel
Designers: Laurie Westdahl, Jennifer Wiezel
Production Artist: Susie Hornig

Typographer: Communication Graphics

Illustrations created in cooperation with Comm-Spot.
Design: Bartholomew
Art Direction: Ronald J. Garnier, Thomas Karleskint
Inking: Susan Launis
Coloring: Linda Hanney, Susie Hornig
Lettering: Linda Hanney

0-8499-8608-7
890123 RRD 987654321

Because you are a human being, you have certain rights.

Every Kid's Guide To Understanding Human Rights will help you learn about

■ the right to be yourself,
■ the right to be honest,
■ the right to have your basic needs met,
■ the right to ask questions and receive honest answers,
■ the right to think your own thoughts and believe your own beliefs,
■ the right to make mistakes,
■ the right to contribute to any decision that affects you,
■ the right to have your own belongings,
■ the right to have privacy,
■ the right to live free from fear,
■ the right to grow and develop at your own pace, and
■ the right to defend your rights.

You have the right to be yourself.

Sometimes the people around you wish you were different. But you cannot be everything other people want you to be. You can only be the person you are.

These are some of the things that make you the person you are:

- what you like,
- what interests you,
- what you think and believe,
- what makes you laugh,
- how you show your feelings,
- how you feel and act around people,
- what you do well and do not do well,
- what your good and bad habits are,
- whether or not you do what you say you will do,
- whether or not you like to work,
- whether you are neat or messy, and
- whether you do things quickly or slowly.

You have the right to be honest.

Sometimes you are asked to say something that is not true. Be thoughtful and kind, but be honest.

Sometimes you are asked to say you are sorry when you are not sorry. Be honest in a kind way.

Sometimes you are asked to say you like something when you don't like it. Be honest in a kind way.

Sometimes you are asked to say yes when you want to say no. Be honest in a kind way.

Sometimes you are asked to say you do not care when you do care. Be honest in a kind way.

Sometimes you are expected to say you understand
something when you don't understand it. Be honest in
a kind way.

Sometimes you are expected to say you feel a way you do not feel. Be honest in a kind way.

Sometimes you are expected to agree when you do not agree. Be honest in a kind way.

You have the right to have your basic needs met.

There are many things you need in order to survive and grow. Do whatever is necessary to make sure you get what you need without hurting yourself or anyone else.

Respect your physical needs. Be sure you get the food, water, exercise, and rest your body needs.

Respect your emotional needs. Accept your feelings.
Express your feelings and respond to them in ways
that do not hurt yourself or others.

Respect your social needs. Develop relationships with other people that are good for both you and them.

Respect your creative needs. Give yourself a chance to do many different things. Try doing things that you have not done before.

Respect your intellectual needs. Allow yourself to be curious. Explore and discover things. Do whatever you can to continue learning.

You have the right to ask questions and receive honest answers.

You must be able to ask questions and receive honest answers so you can learn and grow. Sometimes it is difficult to get answers to your questions. If the people you ask do not know the answers to your questions, find another way to get the answers.

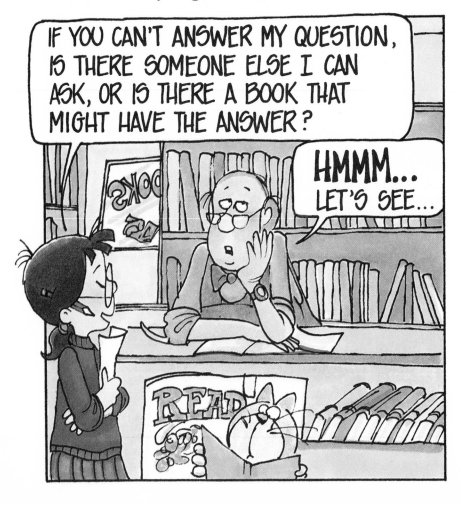

If someone does not want to answer your questions,
ask another person.

If someone is too busy to answer your questions, ask the questions later when the person is not busy.

Do not believe people when they tell you your questions are not important. Your questions do not have to be important to others in order to be important to you.

Do not believe people when they tell you that you are too young to understand. Realize that age does not matter when you want to find out about something. No matter how young or old you are, you can learn about whatever you want to know.

Do not believe people when they tell you that you do not need to know something. Realize that it is important to respond to your curiosity. It is important to find out about things that cause you to wonder. This is how you learn.

You have the right to think your own thoughts and believe your own beliefs.

You think a certain way. Other people might not agree with you. This is OK. You do not need to think the way everyone else does. It is important for you to think your own thoughts.

You believe certain things. Other people might not agree with you. It makes no difference whether or not people agree with you. You must believe what you think is true.

You have the right to make mistakes.

Like every other person in the world, you are not perfect. Sometimes you have accidents and make wrong choices and mistakes. Although these situations are embarrassing and painful, they can help you learn and become a better person.

When you have had an accident, learn to be more careful.

When you have made a wrong choice, learn to get help from other people. Also, think carefully before you make another choice.

When you have made a mistake, use the experience
to learn more about yourself and how you can live your
life more successfully.

You have the right to contribute to any decision that affects you.

Sometimes other people think they know what you should do. Remember, what you think is important too. Share your thoughts and feelings with anyone who wants to decide what you should do.

Sometimes other people think they know how you should look. Remember, what you think is important too. Share your thoughts and feelings with anyone who wants to decide how you should look.

Sometimes other people think they know who you should be with. Remember, what you think is important too. Share your thoughts and feelings with anyone who wants to decide who you should be with.

Sometimes other people think they know what should be done with things that are yours. Your things belong to you. What you think should be done with them is important too. Share your thoughts and feelings with anyone who wants to decide what should be done with your things.

You have the right to have your own belongings.

Things are yours if
- you received them as gifts,
- you made or created them,
- you earned the money to buy them, or
- you traded something for them.

You own your belongings. As long as you do not hurt yourself or anyone else, do whatever you want with them. You can

■ use them,

■ save them,

■ share them, or

■ insist that no one else use them.

Because your belongings are yours, you are responsible for taking care of them. Do not

■ misuse them or

■ lend them to people who might abuse them.

You have the right to privacy.

Sometimes you want to be alone. You want to think and daydream. You want to do something without being distracted or disturbed. It's OK to go someplace where you can be by yourself. Choose a safe place. Tell others where you are going so no one thinks you are lost.

Sometimes you have thoughts or feelings you do not want to share with anyone else. It's OK for you to keep these thoughts and feelings to yourself until you are ready to share them with a trustworthy person.

You have the right to live free from fear.

Sometimes someone or something might cause you to be afraid all the time. It is not good for you to be constantly afraid. If you are afraid of something or someone, you should get some help.

Talk to someone about your fears. Choose a person

■ whom you trust,

■ who cares about you, and

■ who is old enough and wise enough to help you.

The person you talk to might help you see that you have nothing to fear, or the person might help you do something about the cause of your fear.

You have the right to grow and develop at your own pace.

Sometimes other people want you to think and act as if you were an adult. Remember, you are not an adult. So, it is impossible for you to think and act as if you were an adult.

It takes a long time to become an adult. Be patient with yourself. Allow yourself to grow up a little at a time.

Every person is different and grows at his or her own pace. Don't be discouraged if you seem to take longer than other people to grow up. Don't compare yourself to other people.

You have the right to defend your rights.

Sometimes people might not respect your rights. Talk to them about this. Tell them in a kind way exactly how you think and feel. Ask them to be more considerate of your rights.

If these people do not respond to you, get help. Talk to someone who is old enough and wise enough to help you. The person you talk to might help you understand why people are sometimes disrespectful towards you. The person might help you deal with them.

The rights you have as a human being also belong to other people. This means you have a responsibility toward others.

If you want to be your own person, you must allow other people to be their own persons.

If you want to be honest, you must allow other people to be honest.

If you want to have your needs met, you must allow other people to have their needs met.

If you want to ask questions and receive honest answers, you must allow other people to ask questions and receive honest answers.

If you want to think your own thoughts and believe your own beliefs, you must allow other people to think their own thoughts and believe their own beliefs.

If you want to make mistakes, you must allow other people to make mistakes.

If you want to contribute to the decisions that affect you, you must allow other people to contribute to the decisions that affect them.

If you want to have your own belongings, you must allow other people to have their own belongings.

If you want to have privacy, you must allow other people to have privacy.

If you want to live a life free from fear, you must allow other people to live their lives free from fear.

If you want to grow and develop at your own pace, you must allow other people to grow and develop at their own paces.

If you want to defend your rights, you must allow other people to defend their rights.

Your rights make it possible for you to become the wonderful person you were meant to be. This is also true for every other person around you.